DEER
Growing Up in the Wild

A white-tailed fawn curls up in the leaves.

by Judith E. Rinard

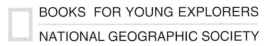
BOOKS FOR YOUNG EXPLORERS
NATIONAL GEOGRAPHIC SOCIETY

Copyright © 1991 National Geographic Society Library of Congress CIP Data: p. 32

At the edge of the woods, late in the spring, two little deer have been born. The baby deer are called fawns and have spotted coats. One fawn drinks its mother's milk. The other snuggles close to its mother. Now the fawns are small and weak. Their mothers will feed them and keep them safe as they grow.

By late summer, fawns are growing fast.
One fawn in a meadow cries out for its mother.
While she is away, the spots on the fawn
help it hide in the grass.

Look how big these hungry twins are getting!
They have to bend their front legs
when their mother feeds them.

There are many kinds of deer in North
America. These are called white-tailed deer.
Can you guess why?

A young deer munches on leaves. It is growing older and has lost its spots. It eats grass and the leaves, twigs, and buds of trees. This deer has big ears like a mule's. It is called a mule deer.

Look closely at these young male deer, called bucks. What do you see on their heads? When the males are a year old, they grow their first set of antlers. Only members of the deer family have antlers, which are made of bone. Each winter, the antlers fall off. The bucks grow a new set in the spring.

At first, antlers look like two small bumps. Then they grow longer and look like fuzzy spikes. In a buck's second year, the spikes begin to grow out like branches.

By his third year, a buck has full-grown antlers. The soft, fuzzy skin that covers them, called velvet, peels off. The peeling looks bloody, but it doesn't hurt the buck. Now the antlers are hard and have sharp points. Another buck rubs his head on a tree, leaving his smell. The smell tells other bucks to stay away. If another buck comes near, what do you think will happen?

Crash! Two bucks ram their antlers together. They are fighting to win a female deer, called a doe. Bucks push and shove to see which one is stronger. The stronger buck will win the doe. Usually, neither buck is killed or even badly hurt.

Listen! What's that? A noise
has scared this white-tailed buck,
and he leaps away. Maybe it's a bear.
Maybe it's a hunter with a gun!

The buck's tail stands straight up.
The snow-white hairs spread out
like a fan. This makes a bright signal
for other deer to see. It says,
"Danger! Run, run, run!"

Deer can see and hear very well.
Strong legs help them run from enemies.
When running, a white-tailed deer
can leap across a country road.

Winter is a hard time for deer. Snow covers the ground, and food is scarce. A buck digs in the snow with his hooves to find grass to eat. Another buck has lost one antler. It may have landed in the snow. The other will soon fall off, too. If deer live near your home, you may see antlers on the ground in the winter.

CARIBOU

Caribou splash across an icy river in Alaska. Each spring, this kind of deer travels in large groups on a long journey north to summer feeding grounds. A mother watches her calf, which was born along the way. It keeps up with the group, or herd, just hours after birth!

In fall, the herd travels south to warmer lands. Thousands of caribou travel together. They are the only kind of deer with antlers on both the males and the females.

ELK

In a mountain meadow,
a mother elk nuzzles her baby,
called a calf. Like caribou, elk
are large deer that live in herds.
The calves are born in spring.

A male elk, called a bull, has big, handsome antlers. In fall, he shows them off to win mates. He makes loud, trumpeting cries and uses his antlers to fight other bulls.

The winning bull becomes leader of a group of females, or cows. Soon his group will join a big herd of elk. They will travel down from the mountains to the valley to find food in winter.

MOOSE

A mother moose guards her twin
babies. Unlike fawns, moose calves
have no spots to camouflage them.
Their mother will fiercely attack
any enemy that comes near,
even a wolf or a bear.

Moose are the largest members of
the deer family. They live in northern
forests near lakes and streams.
At first, the calves are clumsy.
Their legs are wobbly and seem
too long for their bodies.

As it grows, a moose becomes very strong.
It is at home on land or in the water. This
female, or cow, is feeding on water plants
in a lake. A moose is a good swimmer
and can dive deep for favorite plants.
It can swim nonstop for several miles.

A bull moose shakes his head after a swim.
He grows bigger antlers each year.
The largest ones may spread almost as wide
as the moose is tall.

Full grown, a bull moose is huge.
His shoulders may be nearly as high
as the top of a doorway. No longer
a clumsy baby, he is now a mighty giant.

Published by
The National Geographic Society, Washington, D.C.
Gilbert M. Grosvenor, *President*
  and Chairman of the Board
Michela A. English, *Senior Vice President*
Robert L. Breeden, *Executive Adviser to the President*
  for Publications and Educational Media

Prepared by
The Book Division
William R. Gray, *Director*
Margery G. Dunn, *Senior Editor*

Staff for this book
Jane H. Buxton, *Managing Editor*
Charles E. Herron, *Illustrations Editor*
Jody Bolt, *Art Director*
Patricia F. Frakes, Gail N. Hawkins, *Researchers*
Artemis S. Lampathakis, *Illustrations Assistant*
Karen F. Edwards, Sandra F. Lotterman,
  Teresita Cóquia Sison, Marilyn J. Williams,
  Staff Assistants

Engraving, Printing, and Product Manufacture
George V. White, *Director*, and Vincent P. Ryan,
  Manager, Manufacturing and Quality Management
Heather Guwang, *Production Project Manager*
Lewis R. Bassford, Richard S. Wain, *Production*

Consultants
William A. Xanten, Jr., National Zoological Park,
  Smithsonian Institution, *Scientific Consultant*
Peter L. Munroe, *Educational Consultant*
Lynda Bush, *Reading Consultant*

Illustrations Credits
Alan & Sandy Carey (cover); Leonard Lee Rue III/
DRK PHOTO (1); Daniel J. Cox (2, 4, 4-5, 8 left, 8 right,
10, 17 lower, 22-23, 32); Peter McLeod/FIRST LIGHT
(3); Raymond Gehman (6-7); Leonard Lee Rue III/
RUE ENTERPRISES (8-9, 14-15); Len Rue, Jr./
RUE ENTERPRISES (11, 12-13); Tom Mangelsen (16);
Ted Schmoll/PHOTO NETWORK (17 upper);
Stephen J. Krasemann/DRK PHOTO (18 upper, 28);
George F. Mobley, N. G. Photographer (18-19);
Johnny Johnson/DRK PHOTO (20-21); © 1991
Michael Frye (24); Tom & Pat Leeson (25);
Steven C. Kaufman (26-27, 30-31); George J. Sanker/
DRK PHOTO (28-29).

Library of Congress ℂℙ Data
Rinard, Judith E.
  Deer growing up in the wild / by Judith E. Rinard.
    p. cm. — (Books for young explorers)
  Includes bibliographical references.
  Summary: Describes how baby deer are reared in the wild and some of the hardships
they, and other animals like them, encounter.
  ISBN 0-87044-843-9 (regular edition) — ISBN 0-87044-848-X (library edition)
  1. Deer—Juvenile literature. [1. Deer.] I. Title. II. Series.
QL737.U55R56 1991
599.73′57—dc20
                                        91-13502
                                          ℂℙ
                                          AC

In the evening, a white-tailed doe and her fawn wander along a creek to drink.

Cover: Sitting motionless, a white-tailed fawn hides in the grass. Spots on its coat look like patches of sunlight on the ground and make the fawn hard to see.

More About DEER
Growing Up in the Wild

Among the earth's most common large mammals, deer live on every continent but Antarctica. There are more than 60 species of deer. Pictured in this book are deer native to North America, including white-tailed deer—the most abundant—mule deer, elk, caribou, and moose. White-tailed deer range over most of the continent. Mule deer live mainly in the western half of it. Elk are found primarily in the Rocky Mountains and along the northwest coast of the U.S. Caribou range over much of Canada and Alaska. Moose, the largest of all deer, live in Canada and in Alaska and other northern states.

Most female deer give birth to one or sometimes two babies (2, 3, 5, 23, 26, 32).* The fawns stay hidden for their first weeks of life. As they grow, fawns often play, chasing and butting each other. They remain with their mother for about a year. She usually chases

* Numbers in parentheses refer to pages in *Deer Growing Up in the Wild.*

them off when she is about to give birth again. In the wild, deer may live 10 to 20 years.

Deer are browsing animals that eat mostly leaves, buds, and twigs of trees, but they also feed on grasses and nuts. In winter they may paw away snow to find grass or other plants (16). Deer are ruminants, or cud-chewers. They bite off some food and swallow it nearly whole. Later, when they are hidden and resting, they bring up a ball of partly digested food— the cud—and chew it thoroughly.

Deer are the only animals with antlers, which many people confuse with horns. Horns, such as those of goats and antelopes, grow from the skin. They are permanent and continue to grow unless cut off or broken. Antlers are true bones that grow from the skull and fall off each year (17). As they grow, antlers

Looking for food, a hungry moose pokes its head in a restaurant window in Homer, Alaska. In some areas, moose, elk, and other deer may come near people, particularly in cold winter months when plant food is hard to find.

STEVEN C. KAUFMAN

DON & PAT VALENTI / DRK PHOTO (LEFT); STEPHEN J. KRASEMANN / DRK PHOTO (BELOW)

*Huge antlers covered with soft
skin called velvet crown
a male caribou (right). Only
members of the deer family grow
antlers, structures made of bone.
A hoofed animal called a
pronghorn (below) has horns,
which have a bony core that is
encased in a hard material also
found in hair and nails.
The pronghorn differs from other
horned animals in that it sheds
the covering of its horns each year.*

are tender and are covered with soft skin called velvet (8-9, 10). It contains blood vessels that nourish the developing bone. Mature antlers are hard, with branches that end in sharp points, or tines (10-11).

Many deer migrate between summer and winter feeding grounds. Caribou are the champion travelers among deer. They form vast herds of up to tens of thousands. Each year, the herds migrate some 800 miles between their summer feeding grounds on the arctic tundra and their winter homes in forests to the south (18-19, 20-21).

Additional Reading

A First Look at Animals With Horns, by Millicent E. Selsam and Joyce Hunt. (New York, Walker and Co., 1989). Ages 4-8 and up.

Deer, Moose, Elk and Their Family, by Marie M. Jenkins. (New York, Holiday House, Inc., 1979). Ages 8 and up.

Fawn in the Woods, by Irmengarde Eberle. (New York, Thomas Y. Crowell Co., 1962). Ages 8-12.